Facilitation Skills Inventory (FSI)

Observer Guide

Ingrid Bens, M.Ed.

Pfeiffer
A Wiley Imprint
www.pfeiffer.com

Published by Pfeiffer
An Imprint of Wiley
989 Market Street, San Francisco, CA 94103-1741
www.pfeiffer.com

For additional copies/bulk purchases of this book in the U.S. please contact 800-274-4434.

Pfeiffer books and products are available through most bookstores. To contact Pfeiffer directly call our Customer Care Department within the U.S. at 800-274-4434, outside the U.S. at 317-572-3985, fax 317-572-4002, or visit www.pfeiffer.com.

Pfeiffer also publishes its books in a variety of electronic formats. Some content that appears in print may not be available in electronic books.

ISBN-13: 978-0-470-18903-0

Acquiring Editor: Holly Allen
Marketing Manager: Tolu Babalola
Director of Development: Kathleen Dolan Davies
Developmental Editor: Susan Rachmeler

Production Editor: Michael Kay
Editor: Rebecca Taff
Manufacturing Supervisor: Becky Morgan

Printed in the United States of America

Printing   10 9 8 7 6 5 4 3 2

Contents

Overview

The *Facilitation Skills Inventory* has been created to provide a structured feedback mechanism for individuals seeking to become capable facilitators. The inventory describes twenty skills essential to effective practice. When this inventory is used as an observation tool, it generates specific feedback that facilitators, operating at any level, can use to improve their skills and create a personal development strategy.

Facilitation is a complex and nuanced capability that requires years of practice to fully master. By providing structure and a vehicle for observer feedback, the *FSI* aims to accelerate the journey to mastery for facilitators working in all fields of endeavor.

The Important Role of the Observer

The most meaningful aspect of the *FSI* is the detailed feedback that it generates. As an expert observer, you will play two important roles:

1. You will attend a facilitated meeting to record observations about the performance of the facilitator being evaluated and will then translate these observations into ratings

2. You will provide feedback about your ratings and your observations to the facilitator to help him or her identify personal improvement strategies.

Observer Profile

While the *FSI* may be taken by individuals of all skill levels, observers must be experienced facilitators. Because there are so many pathways into facilitation, it's impossible to dictate any specific level of education or number of years in practice.

This is further complicated by the fact that someone who has been a facilitator for years but rarely practices may, in fact, be less expert than someone who's relatively new to the field but who has taken part in formal training and who facilitates on a regular basis.

Ideally, *FSI* observers should have taken part in some formal training and have practiced frequently for at least two to three years. Individuals who have taken part in some form of professional certification program are, of course, ideal.

The bottom line is that observers must themselves be able to perform the skills described in the inventory and rank at the advanced level. (See the *FSI* Skill Levels section that follows and the Cut Scores section later in this Guide.)

The *FSI* Skill Levels

To help organizations and individuals identify the level of skill that matches their circumstances, the *FSI* can be used to identify three distinct skill levels.

Level I—The Developing Facilitator

When individuals first begin to facilitate, they generally start by leading the regularly scheduled staff meetings that are held within their own departments or teams. These are meetings at which they know the members of the group and are also familiar with the content under discussion.

In these meetings the group's leader is typically present, as are the facilitator's peers. These facilitators may be asked in advance to lead the meeting but are often pressed into service without advance notice as the need for structure materializes.

Since more and more leaders are now gaining facilitation skills, it's becoming more common for them to facilitate their staff meetings. This may require them to shift in and then out of the process leader role, as they move from segment to segment of their staff meetings.

People who are relatively new to facilitation or practice it infrequently and who may not have attended formal facilitator training are described in the *FSI* as being at the developing stage.

Developing Facilitators are typically able to:

- Ask basic questions and paraphrase group member comments;

- Call on people to engage them in the conversation;

- Help groups stay on track;

- Use simple decision-making tools such as voting;

- Take notes that reflect the conversation; and

- Summarize ideas to bring closure to discussions.

For a more complete snapshot of the skills demonstrated by the developing facilitator, please refer to the descriptors at the left end of continuum of each of the twenty observable skills of the *FSI*.

While the contribution of the developing facilitator may be very helpful, individuals who operate at this level will also exhibit some or all of the following:

They may appear unsure or nervous. They may fail to provide an effective framework for group discussions or be unable to manage interpersonal dynamics. At times they may fail to keep track of member comments, miss opportunities to question effectively, or even slip out of the neutral role. If the discussion becomes side-tracked, they may be at a loss for strategies to refocus. They may lack process tools for some discussions or provide only a cursory review, so that group members leave their sessions without a sense of closure or clear next steps.

Individuals who score in the developing range on the *FSI* will not be awarded a certificate.

Level II—The Accomplished Facilitator

Having gained experience leading regular staff meetings, the facilitator may be asked to conduct special purpose meetings such as problem-solving sessions, planning meetings, or team-building workshops. This facilitator may conduct these sessions for his or her work group or he or she may be asked to help an outside team.

When a facilitator branches out to design and manage special-purpose discussions, a new set of skills is required. For most practitioners, some formal facilitation training is needed to acquire the tools and techniques needed at this level.

Accomplished Facilitators are typically able to:

- Use a wide variety of process tools and techniques;

- Use norms to set a climate of openness and trust;

- Paraphrase member comments accurately;

- Manage complex group dynamics;

- Remain calm and composed;

- Manage even challenging situations without losing neutrality;

- Use more complex decision-making tools such as decision grids;

- Keep track of far-ranging conversations; and

- Build consensus and create closure.

For a more complete snapshot of the skills demonstrated by the accomplished facilitator, please refer to the mid-point description for each of the twenty observable skills on the FSI.

The accomplished facilitator has growing confidence and comes to meetings prepared to share tools and techniques that help structure discussions. Accomplished facilitators keep proceedings on track and maintain an appropriate pace. They notice ineffective behaviors and intervene with confidence. They do not slip out of the neutral role and they manage participation so that all voices are heard. They provide clear summaries and help members achieve closure. Group members leave their sessions feeling that the facilitator was an asset to their meeting.

Level III—The Advanced Facilitator

After managing a variety of assignments for a diverse mix of groups over a number of years, some facilitators progress to the advanced level of mastery.

While the advanced facilitator may still lead regular staff meetings, individuals operating at this skill level are typically engaged in leading complex projects or designing conversations associated with planned change initiatives. Advanced facilitators also use their skills to conduct team-building sessions and to help clients overcome conflicts.

Advanced Facilitators are typically able to:

- Link a variety of tools and techniques to create coherent process designs;
- Help members set the norms they need for specific situations;
- Surface resistance and help build member buy-in;
- Ask questions that effectively encourage deeper thought;
- Maintain an effective pace without losing personal energy;
- Record key points without losing track of anyone's ideas; and
- Provide clear summaries that accurately reflect all views.

For a more complete snapshot of the skills demonstrated by the advanced facilitator, please refer to the descriptions at the right end of the continuum on each of twenty observable skills of the *FSI*.

Advanced facilitators are calm and confident, even in stressful situations. They know how to safely surface resistance and build member buy-in. When a challenging situation arises, they know how to reestablish a positive climate and refocus without losing their neutrality. The advanced facilitator knows how to structure complex decision-making conversations using a wide range of tools.

Regardless of how wide-ranging the conversation, the advanced facilitator can keep track of all salient points and provide members with a comprehensive summary of the discussion. Group members leave a session led by an advanced facilitator feeling that he or she made a major contribution to the success of the proceedings.

The *FSI* Competencies

So how can you use the FSI to determine the skill level of a facilitator? By observing and rating the facilitator on twenty selected behaviors. These behaviors were selected based on a three-round evaluation process conducted by subject-matter experts. Further information about the development and testing process for the *FSI* can be found in white paper posted online at www.pfeiffer.com/go/facilitationskills.

The twenty questions of the *FSI* are organized into four competency categories:

- Core skills
- Personal deportment
- Group management
- Process management

Core skills refers to those practices that are at the heart of facilitation and that are in use during all facilitated activities. The core skills that have been selected for observation are

1. Staying neutral
2. Asking questions
3. Paraphrasing
4. Note-taking
5. Summarizing

Personal deportment refers to the outward demeanor and behaviors exhibited by facilitators. The elements of personal deportment that have been selected for observation are

6. Personal demeanor
7. Attending behavior
8. Body language
9. Focus
10. Personal energy

Group management refers to those skills that facilitators use to create and maintain effective interactions. The elements of group management that have been selected for observation are

11. Setting the climate
12. Gaining buy-in
13. Fostering participation
14. Managing digressions
15. Managing conflict

Process management refers to the ability to appropriately deploy process tools and techniques in order to provide structure to interactions. The elements of process management that have been selected for observation are

16. Designing process agendas

17. Presenting parameters

18. Structuring decision making

19. Process checking

20. Creating closure

Cut Scores

Each skill on the *FSI* has been given two "cut" scores, which indicate the rating one must achieve on that skill to be considered either "Accomplished" or "Advanced." The cut scores are included on the Scoring Sheet on page 20. However, you should not let these numbers influence your ratings on the *FSI*.

The cut scores were arrived at based on evaluation by subject-matter experts using the Angoff technique. (Again, see the white paper posted at www.pfeiffer.com/go/facilitationskills for further detail.)

While all twenty of the skills in the inventory are important, four skills have been judged by a panel of experts to be crucial. (See the discussion on non-substitutability in the Appendix.) These four skills are at the heart of the facilitator role and must be strongly in evidence.

These four essential skills are

1. Staying Neutral

2. Asking Questions

3. Paraphrasing

16. Designing Process Agendas

In the case of these four skills, high performance thresholds have been set in the rating process. Individuals who do not score at or above the set cut score on *all four* critical elements will not be deemed to be in the specified category, regardless of their total scores.

If, for example, an individual attains an overall score that is above the overall total for the Accomplished Facilitator level, but scores below the Accomplished Facilitator cut line on even one of the four essential elements, the person will not be certified to be at that level.

Let's consider neutrality. Even if an individual scores well in the other nineteen skills, can he or she really be said to be facilitating effectively if he or she periodically lapses out of neutrality? Because the answer is no, the cut score for staying neutral has been set at 5.0 for anyone seeking to be certified at the advanced level.

The following information is provided to shed more light on the matter of the cut scores in the four essential skills:

1. Staying neutral—Because facilitation is by definition a neutral role, it is essential that facilitators remain consistently neutral. For this reason, the cut scores for this item are very high. Staying neutral means knowing how to ask questions in a manner that doesn't take decision-making power away from group members. It also means being able to introduce helpful content suggestions in a way that doesn't influence members to make a particular decision. Observers are asked to take special notice of the extent to which the facilitator manages to remain neutral.

2. Asking questions—The most foundational ability of effective facilitators is their ability to ask effective questions. Facilitators use questions to clarify ideas and to guide deeper inquiry. Asking the right questions is an art. Observers are asked to notice whether or not the facilitator's questions help focus conversation or drive it into unrelated areas. Do the person ask enough questions at the right time?

3. Paraphrasing—Facilitators must be active listeners who can demonstrate their attentiveness by continuously feeding back member comments. Experienced practitioners paraphrase continuously to acknowledge that they have heard member ideas and to clarify meaning. They also use paraphrasing to defuse emotions when managing conflict situations. Observers are asked to notice whether facilitators are paraphrasing accurately and frequently enough. Is the paraphrasing accurate, or does the facilitator change the meaning of ideas when feeding them back to members?

16. Designing process agendas—One of the greatest contributions of process leaders is that they provide structure to interactions so that the participants can focus on the content. Inexperienced practitioners often lack the ability to link tools and techniques together for form a coherent framework for discussions. Experienced facilitators spend time before a facilitated session to research and prepare a blueprint. If pre-work isn't possible, they take time at the start of a discussions to lay out a clear process pathway. Observers are asked to notice whether or not the facilitator appears to be working from a process design. Does the facilitator clearly describe tools and steps to group members? Does he or she systematically move members through the process that was described?

The Observation Process

The following section provides some information about the observation process and guidelines for the most effective way to conduct your observations.

Pre-Work

You will need to take at least an hour prior to the observed session to thoroughly review this Guide and familiarize yourself with the *Facilitation Skills Inventory*.

Get in touch with the facilitator and other observers (if there are any) to determine where and when you'll meet for the final feedback session. Although it's important to meet promptly after the observed session (while the session is still fresh in everyone's mind), you will need to allow some time (approximately thirty minutes; more if there are multiple observers) between the observed session and the feedback session to prepare for the feedback session.

The Observed Session

The facilitated session that you will observe will be a real meeting, not a simulation or role play. It should last a minimum of ninety minutes. Although attendees will be aware of the purpose of your presence, you will be sitting away from the table and should not intrude on the session in any way. If there are other observers in attendance, please do not speak to one another during the session.

The Tasks

During the session, you will observe the facilitator, look for behaviors described in the *FSI*, and record your observations and thoughts on the Observation Sheets. There are three sheets—labeled "start," "middle," and "end."

The start includes anything that the facilitator does to establish the parameters of the session. Start elements should not take more than the first fifteen or twenty minutes.

The end will most likely also take between fifteen and twenty minutes. This is sufficient time for the facilitator to provide a clear summary, test consensus, help members identify next steps, and so on.

Throughout the session, take detailed notes on the facilitator's performance. Never rely on your memory of events. As you will see from the examples provided, it's important to record the details of specific incidents—and even what the facilitator said to respond.

You will *not* fill out the *FSI* during the session, only the Observer Sheets.

Observer Demeanor Guidelines

- Maintain neutral facial expressions and avoid scowling or looking displeased, as this may undermine the facilitator's confidence.
- Work hard to observe without making eye contact with the facilitator.
- Do not speak up, interject comments, or otherwise draw attention to yourself.

The Scoring Process

At the end of the observed session, allow at least half an hour to reflect on your personal observations and rate the facilitator prior to the feedback session. If there are multiple observers, you'll need additional time to compare observations and arrive at an aggregate rating.

To begin the scoring process, privately review your personal observations and use those observations to complete the *FSI*, rating the performance of the facilitator on each of the twenty skills described in the inventory.

Note that each scale has been broken into quarters. Place your marks on top of these dividers and not in the spaces between. Do not mark scores using an X. Use a simple vertical line as per the example below:

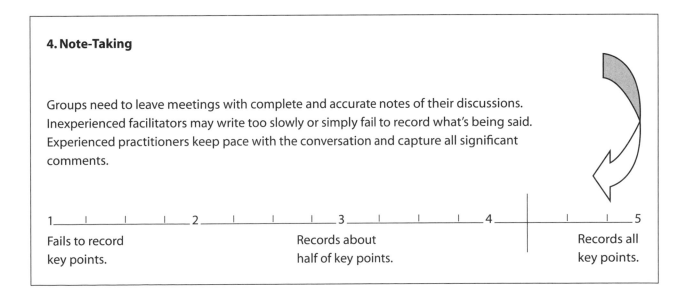

4. Note-Taking

Groups need to leave meetings with complete and accurate notes of their discussions. Inexperienced facilitators may write too slowly or simply fail to record what's being said. Experienced practitioners keep pace with the conversation and capture all significant comments.

1————|————|————|————2————|————|————|————3————|————|————|————4————|————|————|————5

Fails to record   Records about   Records all
key points.   half of key points.   key points.

It's important to complete the scoring of the twenty skills immediately after the facilitated session so that important details are not forgotten.

Once you've completed the FSI, transfer your scores to the Scoring Sheet and sum the sub-totals for each of the four categories and then determine the overall total.

If there are multiple observers, each of you will be filling out the *FSI* and the Scoring Sheet separately. One the individual scoring is complete, you and the other observers should share your observations and arrive at the final scores, You can do this by averaging your individual ratings (an averaging worksheet is provided in this Guide), but detailed discussion in which each of you explains your ratings is a superior approach. This allows each of you to explain the rationale behind your scores and can help eliminate erroneous ratings that were based on mistaken assumptions or misperceptions.

When there are multiple raters, it's very important that the facilitator hear only the aggregate score and that no single observer share his or her personal ratings in a way that undermines the official tally.

Prior to meeting with the facilitator, you should also review your notes and think about suggestions you might make to the facilitator to improve his or her performance. If there are multiple raters, you can discuss improvement suggestions as a group.

The Feedback Process

Meet with the facilitator and the other observers (if there are any) at the predetermined place and time.

Step 1—Begin by asking the facilitator to describe what he or she felt that he or she did well during the session. At this stage, do not allow the facilitator to talk about his or her perception of the weaknesses of the performance, only the strengths.

Step 2—The observers then take turns telling the facilitator what they saw him or her do well. You should refer to your Observation Sheets and provide as many specific examples of effective actions as possible.

Step 3—Once all of the strengths have been shared, invite the facilitator to reflect on what he or she could have done better.

Step 4—After the facilitator has identified his or her weaknesses, share your suggestions for ways the facilitator could improve his or her performance. Comments should be focused on what the facilitator could do to be even more effective, rather than on what he or she did wrong. Some examples:

Instead of saying, *"Writing in red was a mistake,"* offer a tip like, *"Using dark markers will make your notes easier to read."*

Instead of saying, *"You forgot to describe the process,"* offer a tip like, *"In the future, take the time to explain the tools and techniques you will be using."*

Instead of saying, *"You didn't notice that some people never spoke,"* offer a tip like, *"Always be on the lookout for people who haven't been heard from."*

At the end of the feedback session, give the facilitator a copy of the Observation Sheets with the detailed notes that you took during the session. The facilitator will want to have these notes for personal development planning. He or she will not need your Scoring Sheet as the facilitator scoring page has a place to record the observer scores.

It's possible that the administrator will want to collect your individual Scoring Sheets. If this is the case, the administrator will let you know how to submit these.

When the process is complete, fill out the Program Evaluation form on page 22 and turn it in to the administrator.

FSI Sample Observation Sheet

While you should review the descriptions of the twenty skills prior to the observed session, the inventory should be put aside during the observed session. Instead, you should use the blank Observation Sheets that are provided starting on page 13 to record your observations. The statements below offer examples of the level of detail that should be recorded.

S	Started with a warm welcome; introduced self, did member intros
	Appeared very calm and confident
T	Reviewed the purpose of the meeting and time frames
A	Did not describe the process or how the discussion would unfold
R	Did not ask about barriers or refer to degree of buy-in
T	Briefly referred to the existing norms posted in the room
	Asked a very effective question to start the discussion

	Called on people by name
	Paraphrased continuously
	Made notes that captured most key ideas
	Did a summary at the end of the first topic
	Asked very good probing questions that helped members dig deeper
	Did appear to be working from a process design
	Managed to offer content suggestions without losing neutrality
M	When challenged about the process, stopped and calmly asked:
I	*"Tell me your concern and let's see if others feel the same."*
D	Flexibly changed the approach being used without looking fazed
D	Stopped and asked: *"How is this going? Are we on track? How's the pace? Is everyone still*
L	*clear about what we're doing?"*
E	Noticed a conflict and redirected effectively: *"I see that we have two different opinions. I want to be sure you're hearing each other's points. Please make your points again and this time would you tell me what you hear the other person saying."*
	Allowed people to digress and didn't bring back focus soon enough
	Stayed neutral throughout
	Never lost track of the conversation or failed to write down key points
	Did not notice or ask about the distracted body language being displayed by some members

	Stayed calm and maintained high personal energy right to the end.
	Gave a very clear and complete summary of all notes
E	Saved time for next step planning
N	Checked buy-in for action plans with all members
D	Ended on a positive note: *"Today's topic wasn't an easy one, so I want to thank you for all of your candor and your hard work to arrive at these action plans. Please do not hesitate to ask me for assistance again."*

Observation Sheet

S
T
A
R
T

Observation Sheet

M
I
D
D
L
E

Observation Sheet

END

Facilitation Skills Inventory: Observer

Core Skills: Practices at the Heart of Facilitation

1. Staying Neutral

Staying neutral on the content of discussions is the hallmark of the facilitator role. Those who are new to facilitation often have difficulty holding back their opinions. Experienced facilitators remain focused on the process without inadvertently straying into the content.

1 —————————— 2 —————————— 3 —————————— 4 —————————— 5

Fails to stay neutral. Repeatedly joins the content conversation.

Mostly neutral, but occasionally joins the content conversation.

Remains neutral to focus on the process.

2. Asking Questions

Questioning is the most fundamental facilitator tool. Inexperienced facilitators commonly fail to question effectively. Experienced facilitators ask questions more frequently and use detailed questioning to challenge, clarify, and probe.

1 —————————— 2 —————————— 3 —————————— 4 —————————— 5

Fails to ask effective questions.

Sometimes asks effective questions.

Consistently asks effective questions.

3. Paraphrasing

Facilitators need to be great listeners who can accurately play back participant comments. Novices often do not paraphrase enough. More experienced practitioners paraphrase continuously to clarify ideas and communicate to group members that they've been heard.

1 —————————— 2 —————————— 3 —————————— 4 —————————— 5

Doesn't paraphrase at all.

Sometimes misses critical opportunities to paraphrase.

Paraphrases appropriately throughout.

4. Note-Taking

Groups need to leave meetings with complete and accurate notes of their discussions. Inexperienced facilitators may write too slowly or simply fail to record what's being said. Experienced practitioners keep pace with the conversation and capture all significant comments.

1 —————————— 2 —————————— 3 —————————— 4 —————————— 5

Fails to record key points.

Records about half of key points.

Records all key points.

5. Summarizing

Summarizing can be used to restart stalled conversations or bring closure to discussions. Novice facilitators often fail to summarize, while experienced practitioners frequently review the points under discussion to integrate comments, ratify decisions, and create closure.

1 —————————— 2 —————————— 3 —————————— 4 —————————— 5

Fails to provide summaries of discussions.

Occasionally summarizes discussions.

Provides effective and timely summaries.

Personal Deportment: Outward Demeanor and Behaviors

6. Personal Demeanor

Facilitating can be challenging. Newcomers may be nervous and unsure, even when progress is smooth. Seasoned practitioners remain calm regardless of what happens, confident in their ability to manage any situation.

1 —————————— 2 —————————— 3 —————————— 4 —————————— 5

Appears nervous or unsure throughout.

Occasionally appears nervous or unsure.

Consistently seems calm and confident.

7. Attending Behavior

Group members often communicate through body language. Experienced facilitators are attuned to non-verbal cues and don't hesitate to ask group members about their thoughts and feelings. Newer facilitators may miss these cues or be reluctant to ask members about their non-verbal gestures.

1 —————————— 2 —————————— 3 —————————— 4 —————————— 5

Fails to pick up on or respond to non-verbal cues.

Occasionally picks up on and responds to non-verbal cues.

Appropriately picks up on and responds to non-verbal cues.

8. Body Language

Experienced facilitators are aware of how their bodily mannerisms, postures, and facial expressions communicate their feeling or psychological state. As a result, the body language or tone of voice they use is always appropriate to the situation. Those who are new to facilitation may be unaware of what they're projecting and may use a tone of voice or body language that doesn't match the situation.

1 —————————— 2 —————————— 3 —————————— 4 —————————— 5

Uses an inappropriate tone of voice or body language throughout.

Occasionally uses an inappropriate tone of voice or body language.

Consistently uses an appropriate tone of voice or body language.

9. Focus

In any discussion, numerous ideas may be in play at the same time. Inexperienced practitioners may lose track of discussion points. Masterful facilitators can listen to and remember numerous comments, even while taking notes and observing member interactions.

1 —————————— 2 —————————— 3 —————————— 4 —————————— 5

Constantly loses track of member comments.

Occasionally loses track of member comments.

Consistently keeps track of all relevant comments.

10. Personal Energy

Facilitating is hard work! Experienced practitioners know how to conserve their energy and remain active throughout their work, while newcomers may become exhausted and drained.

1 —————————— 2 —————————— 3 —————————— 4 —————————— 5

Appears exhausted and drained throughout.

Periodically appears exhausted and drained.

Remains lively and energetic throughout.

Group Management: Skills Needed to Create and Maintain Effective Interactions

11. Setting the Climate

Inexperienced facilitators often do not understand the importance of establishing ground rules or *norms*. As a result, they may lead discussions without engaging members in identifying an appropriate code of conduct. Experienced facilitators always ensure that the norms needed to create a safe and collaborative environment are in place.

1 ——|——|——|—— 2 ——|——|——|—— 3 ——|——|——|—— 4 ——|——|——|—— 5

Fails to help group members create needed norms.	Helps members identify some needed norms.	Helps members identify needed norms.

12. Gaining Buy-In

Lack of buy-in can be a roadblock to full and active participation. Novice facilitators may assume that participants are automatically buying in. Advanced practitioners help members identify blocks and create strategies to overcome barriers to engagement.

1 ——|——|——|—— 2 ——|——|——|—— 3 ——|——|——|—— 4 ——|——|——|—— 5

Fails to help members buy in.	Partially explores member buy-in.	Helps members fully buy in.

13. Fostering Participation

There are many reasons why some people speak up in meetings while others hold back. Inexperienced facilitators may let a few people dominate. Experienced facilitators call on quiet people and use a variety of anonymous and sub-grouping techniques to ensure that all viewpoints are heard.

1 ——|——|——|—— 2 ——|——|——|—— 3 ——|——|——|—— 4 ——|——|——|—— 5

Does not engage everyone.	Occasionally engages everyone.	Continuously engages everyone.

14. Managing Digressions

Any discussion can become sidetracked. Those who are new to facilitation may fail to notice digressions or to bring them to the attention of group members. Skilled facilitators tactfully point out sidetracking and refocus the conversation.

1 ——|——|——|—— 2 ——|——|——|—— 3 ——|——|——|—— 4 ——|——|——|—— 5

Fails to point out digressions or refocus discussions.	Occasionally points out digressions and refocuses discussions.	Consistently points out digressions and refocuses discussions.

15. Managing Conflict

Disagreements and ineffective behaviors can crop up in any meeting. Those who are new to facilitation may fail to notice these instances or avoid dealing with them. Advanced practitioners notice these interactions and use appropriate language to redirect ineffective behaviors.

1 ——|——|——|—— 2 ——|——|——|—— 3 ——|——|——|—— 4 ——|——|——|—— 5

Fails to intervene to redirect ineffective behaviors.	Intervenes about half as often as should.	Intervenes when necessary to redirect ineffective behaviors.

Process Management: Using Tools and Techniques to Provide Structure to Interactions

16. Designing Process Agendas

Providing structure is one of the main contributions of the facilitator. Those who are new to facilitation typically lack the ability to link process tools and techniques to form a blueprint for discussion. Experienced practitioners know how to create a coherent process agenda, which they explain to group members.

1 —————|————|————|—— 2 —————|————|————|—— 3 —————|————|————|—— 4 —————|————|————|—— 5

| Appears to be working without a process design. | Appears to be working with some elements of a process design. | Appears to be working from a coherent process design. |

17. Presenting Parameters

Discussions during which the purpose, process, and timeframes are unclear can easily become confused. Inexperienced facilitators may plunge in without clarifying these parameters. Masterful facilitators always start each discussion by clarifying the purpose or expected outcomes, the process or how discussions will be structured, and how much time is available.

1 —————|————|————|—— 2 —————|————|————|—— 3 —————|————|————|—— 4 —————|————|————|—— 5

| Starts discussions without clarifying the parameters. | Clarifies some of the parameters. | Starts each discussion by clarifying the purpose, process, and timeframe. |

18. Structuring Decision Making

Providing structure for decision making is an important facilitator contribution. Experienced facilitators are aware of the various decision-making tools that are available and are able to deploy the right technique to match each situation. Inexperienced facilitators are often unaware of different approaches or when to use them.

1 —————|————|————|—— 2 —————|————|————|—— 3 —————|————|————|—— 4 —————|————|————|—— 5

| Appears unaware of when to use which decision tool. | Sometimes matches decision tools to the situation. | Consistently matches decision tools to various situations. |

19. Process Checking

Experienced facilitators periodically ask participants whether the purpose of the session is still clear, whether they think the process is working, and whether the pace feels appropriate to them. Inexperienced facilitators often fail to conduct process checks, even when there are signs that things are not going well.

1 —————|————|————|—— 2 —————|————|————|—— 3 —————|————|————|—— 4 —————|————|————|—— 5

| Never stops to conduct process checks. | Conducts some process checks. | Conduct all appropriate process checks. |

20. Creating Closure

Every meeting should end with a review of the points discussed, the decisions made, and agreed-to next steps. Experienced practitioners budget time for closing comments and provide a comprehensive summary. Those who are new to facilitation often fail to plan for this activity or may provide only a cursory review.

1 —————|————|————|—— 2 —————|————|————|—— 3 —————|————|————|—— 4 —————|————|————|—— 5

| Ends without a review of the discussion, decisions made, and next steps. | Closes with a cursory or incomplete review of the discussion, decisions, and next steps. | Ends with a complete review of points discussed, decisions made, and next steps. |

FSI Scoring Sheet

Once each of the twenty skills has been rated, record your scores in the Ratings column. Add the totals for each of the four subsets and record these in the appropriate boxes. Finally, calculate the total score and record that number at the bottom of the sheet.

Skills	Cut Scores Accom.	Adv.	Ratings	Competency Categories
1. Staying Neutral	4.75	5.0		Core Skills Total
2. Asking Questions	3.75	4.25		
3. Paraphrasing	4.0	4.5		
4. Note-Taking	3.5	4.0		
5. Summarizing	3.75	4.25		
6. Personal Demeanor	3.75	4.25		Personal Deportment Total
7. Attending Behavior	3.5	4.0		
8. Body Language	3.5	4.0		
9. Focus	3.5	4.0		
10. Personal Energy	3.5	4.0		
11. Setting the Climate	3.75	4.25		Group Management Total
12. Gaining Buy-In	3.5	4.0		
13. Fostering Participation	3.75	4.25		
14. Managing Digressions	3.5	4.0		
15. Managing Conflict	3.5	4.0		
16. Designing Process Agendas	3.75	4.25		Process Management Total
17. Presenting Parameters	3.25	4.0		
18. Structuring Decision Making	3.5	4.0		
19. Process Checking	3.25	3.75		
20. Creating Closure	3.75	4.25		
Totals (Out of a possible 100)	**73.0**	**83.0**		

Averaging Sheet

If there are multiple observers and you wish to compute the average ratings for the observed session, use the following grid.

For each observer, record the competency category sub-totals and the overall total from the Scoring Sheet. Then, for each category, sum the scores and divide by the number of observers. Do the same for the total score.

Core Skills	Personal Deportment	Group Management	Process Management	Total
Observer 1				
Observer 2				
Observer 3				
Observer 4				
Sum				
Average (= sum/number of observers)				

Program Evaluation

Please provide your feedback about the *FSI* to the test administrator.

Name:_____   Location: _____

Role (check one): _____   ☐ Facilitator

☐ Observer

1. Describe what you most liked about the *FSI* process. What were the most effective or useful elements?

2. Describe what you least liked about the *FSI* process. What were the most difficult or ineffective elements?

3. Describe changes that would improve how the process was conducted.

4. What overall rating would you give this process?

1	2	3	4	5
poor	fair	satisfactory	good	excellent

Please explain your rating:

Suggested Reading

Bens, Ingrid. (2005). *Facilitating with Ease!* San Francisco, CA: Jossey-Bass.

Ghais, Suzanne. (2004). *Extreme Facilitation*. San Francisco, CA: Jossey-Bass.

Hart, Lois. (1992). *Faultless Facilitation*. Amherst, MA: HRD Press.

Hogan, Christine. (2003). *Practical Facilitation*. Sterling, VA: Kogan Page.

Justice, Tom, & Jamieson, David. (2005). *The Facilitator's Fieldbook*. New York: American Management Association.

Kaner, Sam. (1996). *Facilitator's Guide to Participatory Decision-Making*. Philadelphia, PA: New Society Publishers.

Rees, Fran. (1998). *The Facilitator Excellence Handbook*. San Francisco, CA: Pfeiffer. Schwarz, Roger. (2005). *The Skilled Facilitator*. San Fransisco, CA: Jossey-Bass.

Stachan, Dorothy. (2008). *Process Design: Making It Work*. San Francisco, CA: Jossey-Bass.

Stanfield, R.B. (Ed.). (2000). *The Art of Focused Conversation*. Toronto, Ontario, Canada: ICA.

Wilkinson, Michael. (2004). *The Secrets of Facilitation*. San Francisco, CA: Jossey-Bass.

About the Author

Ingrid Bens is a consultant and trainer whose special areas of expertise are facilitation skills, team building, and conflict management. She has a master's degree in adult education and more than twenty-five years of experience as a workshop leader and organization development consultant.

Through her popular facilitation skills workshops, Ms. Bens has trained tens of thousands of facilitators throughout the United States and Canada. She is also the author of three Jossey-Bass publications: *Advanced Facilitation Strategies*, *Facilitating to Lead*, and the best-selling, *Facilitating with Ease!*

She is the principal partner of Participative Dynamics, a consulting firm located in Sarasota, Florida, and the founder of Facilitation Tutor, which provides facilitation skills e-learning on the Internet.